Mark Ravenhill

Over There

Methuen Drama

Published by Methuen Drama 2009

1 3 5 7 9 10 8 6 4 2

Methuen Drama
A & C Black Publishers Limited
36 Soho Square
London W1D 3HB
www.acblack.com

Copyright © 2009 Mark Ravenhill

Mark Ravenhill has asserted his rights under the
Copyright, Designs and Patents Act 1988
to be identified as the author of this work

ISBN: 978 1 408 11953 2

A CIP catalogue record for this book is available
from the British Library

Typeset by Country Setting, Kingsdown, Kent
Printed and bound in Great Britain by
CPI Cox & Wyman, Reading, Berkshire

Caution
All rights whatsoever in this play are strictly reserved
and application for performance etc. should be made before
rehearsals begin to Casarotto Ramsay and Associates Limited,
Waverley House, 7–12 Noel Street, London W1F 8GQ.
No performance may be given unless a licence has been obtained.

All rights reserved. No part of this publication may be reproduced
in any form or by any means – graphic, electronic or mechanical, including
photocopying, recording, taping or information storage and retrieval systems –
without the written permission of A & C Black Publishers Limited.

This book is produced using paper that is made from wood grown in
managed, sustainable forests. It is natural, renewable and recyclable.
The logging and manufacturing processes conform to the environmental
regulations of the country of origin.

ROYAL COURT

The Royal Court Theatre and
Schaubühne am Lehniner Platz, Berlin, present

OVER THERE
by **Mark Ravenhill**

First performance at the Royal Court Jerwood Theatre Downstairs,
Sloane Square, London, on 2 March 2009

First performance at the Schaubühne am Lehniner Platz, Berlin,
on 23 March 2009

OVER THERE is presented as part of International Playwrights: A Genesis Project
with additional support from the Goethe-Institut London

OVER THERE is part of OFF THE WALL, a season of new plays about Germany,
marking the 60th anniversary of the foundation of the Federal Republic
of Germany and the 20th anniversary of the fall of the Berlin Wall.

Co-production with the Schaubühne am Lehniner Platz, Berlin,
as part of 'Germany at 60 – Approaching an Uncomfortable Identity',
supported by the German Cultural Foundation

Genesis
FOUNDATION

OVER THERE
by **Mark Ravenhill**

Cast in order of appearance

Karl **Luke Treadaway**
Franz **Harry Treadaway**

Directed by **Ramin Gray** and **Mark Ravenhill**
Designer **Johannes Schütz**
Lighting Designer **Matt Drury**
Sound Designer **Alex Caplen**
Original Music **Harry Treadaway** and **Luke Treadaway**
Assistant Director **Lydia Ziemke**
Movement **Dominic Leclerc**
Casting Director **Amy Ball**
Production Manager **Paul Handley**
Stage Manager **Bryan Paterson**
Deputy Stage Manager **Sarah Tryfan**
Assistant Stage Manager **Samantha Tooby**
Costumes **Iona Kenrick**
Set built by **Miraculous Engineering**

THE COMPANY

MARK RAVENHILL (Writer/Director)

Mark Ravenhill's plays have been widely performed in both English and German. These include: Shopping and Fucking (Out of Joint/Royal Court and Deutsches Theater Baracke); Some Explicit Polaroids (Out of Joint at the Ambassadors Theatre, Zurich Schauspielhaus), Product (Paines Plough at the Traverse, Schaubühne); The Cut (The Donmar/Schaubühne) and Pool No Water (Frantic Assembly at Lyric Hammersmith/ Zurich Schauspielhaus). His Shoot/Get Treasure/Repeat cycle of plays (Paines Plough/ National Theatre/Royal Court/Gate/Out of Joint) will open in German language theatres next season.

MATT DRURY (Lighting)

FOR THE ROYAL COURT: The Stone, Shades, Birth of a Nation, The Mother.

OTHER THEATRE INCLUDES: Private Lives, Same Time Next Year, Absent Friends, Absurd Person Singular, Deadly Nightcap, Bedroom Farce, Sweet Revenge, Joking Apart, Dead Certain, Cinderella, Dangerous Obsession, Spider's Web (Theatre Royal Windsor); Under Their Hats, (Thorndike Theatre, Leatherhead & West End), Nicholas Nickleby, The Hollow Crown, Guys and Dolls, (Thorndike Theatre, Leatherhead); The Flipside, Shirley Valentine, The Gentle Hook (Bill Kenwright); Fools Rush In (UK Tour); Funny Money (UK Tour); Two of A Kind (UK Tour); Catch Me if You Can (UK Tour); Framed (National); Cassie (Everyman, Cheltenham); Scooping the Pot (UK Tour); Daemons (European Tour); The Hollow (UK Tour), The Unexpected Guest (UK Tour); The Haunted Hotel (UK Tour); Arsenic and Old Lace (UK Tour); An Ideal Husband (UK Tour).

Matt is Head of Lighting at the Royal Court.

RAMIN GRAY (Director)

FOR THE ROYAL COURT: The Stone, The Arsonists, The Ugly One, Scenes from the Back of Beyond, Woman and Scarecrow, Motortown (& Wiener Festwochen), Way to Heaven, Bear Hug, The Weather, Ladybird, Advice to Iraqi Women, Terrorism, Night Owls, Just a Bloke, Push Up, How I Ate a Dog.

OTHER THEATRE INCLUDES: Harper Regan (Salzburger Festspiele/Deutsche Schauspielhaus, Hamburg); I'll Be the Devil (RSC/Tricycle); On the Shore of the Wide World (Volkstheater, Wien); King of Hearts (Hampstead/ Out of Joint); The American Pilot (RSC); The Child, The Invisible Woman (Gate); Cat and Mouse (Sheep) (Théâtre National de l'Odéon, Paris/Gate); A Message for the Broken-Hearted (Liverpool Playhouse/BAC); At Fifty She Discovered the Sea, Harry's Bag, Pig's Ear, A View from the Bridge (Liverpool Playhouse).

OPERA INCLUDES: Death in Venice (Staatsoper Hamburg/Theater an der Wien).

Ramin is an Associate Director of the Royal Court.

ALEX CAPLEN (Sound Designer)

THEATRE INCLUDES: Mine, Ten Tiny Toes, War and Peace (Shared Experience); Stephen and the Sexy Partridge (Old Red Lion); Peter Pan, Holes, Duck Variations (UK Tour), The Wizard of Oz (Nuffield Theatre); Imogen (Oval House/UK Tour).

AS SOUND OPERATOR FOR THE ROYAL COURT: Wig Out!, Rhinoceros, The Arsonists, Free Outgoing, Now or Later and Gone too Far (Hackney Empire).

OTHER THEATRE INCLUDES: Kindertransport (Shared Experience); Blood Brothers (International Tour); Ballroom (UK Tour).

Alex is a member of the Sound Department at the Royal Court.

JOHANNES SCHÜTZ (Designer)

THEATRE INCLUDES (in collaboration with Jürgen Gosch): Wer hat Angst vor Virginia Woolf? Zurüstung für die Unsterblichkeit (Deutsches Theater Berlin); Kätchen von Heilbronn, Bakchen (Düsseldorfer Schauspielhaus); Le Maman et la Putain, Die Stunde da wir nichts voneinander wußten, Die Möwe, Endspiel (Bochum Schauspielhaus).

OTHER THEATRE INCLUDES: A Streetcar Named Desire (Theater an der Wien); Tristan und Isolde (Direction and design, Staatstheater Kassel); Antonius und Kleopatra (Bochum Schauspielhaus); Das harte Brot (Schauspielhaus Zürich); Merlin (Münchner Kammerspiele).

DANCE INCLUDES: Extensive work with Reinhild Hoffman including Erwartung/Pierrot Lunaire (Theater am Goetheplatz, Bremen); Zeche Eins (Schauspeilhaus, Bochum); Idomeneo (Direction with R. Hoffmann and stage/costume design, Oper Frankfurt).

OPERA INCLUDES: Jenufa and The Coronation of Poppea (Deutsche Oper am Rhein, Düsseldorf); Die Entführung aus dem Serail (Staatstheater Kassel); Extensive work with Peter Mussbach including Parsifal, Das Schloss (Opéra de La Monnaie, Brussels); Barber of Seville (Oper, Frankfurt).

AWARDS INCLUDE: 2007 Gold Medal Prague; 2005 Costume Designer of the Year and Quadriennale for scenography and costume for Macbeth; 2005 Stage Designer of the Year for stage design for Summerfolk.

HARRY TREADAWAY

TELEVISION INCLUDES: The Shooting of Thomas Hurndall, Cape Wrath, Recovery, Miss Marple: Sleeping Murder, After Life.

FILM INCLUDES: Pelican Blood, Fish Tank, Love You More, City of Ember, The Disappeared, Control, Brothers of the Head.

LUKE TREADAWAY

THEATRE INCLUDES: Cradle Me (Finborough); Piranha Heights (Soho); War Horse, Saint Joan (National).

TELEVISION INCLUDES: Clapham Junction, The Innocence Project.

FILM INCLUDES: Heartless, Viko, Dogging: A Love Story, God's Wounds, Brothers of the Head.

RADIO INLCUDES: Caligari, War Horse.

LYDIA ZIEMKE (Assistant Director)

AS ASSISTANT DIRECTOR FOR THE ROYAL COURT: The Stone

AS DIRECTOR: The Night before Christmas (translation & reading Schaubühne); Stamped (Theatre 503); Lilo's Lido & Thrown (nightmare before valentine/IUGTE International Theatre Methods Festival, Latvia); WEG-A WAY (Schaubühne/ Contacting the World Festival, Liverpool); Reap what you sow (Young Vic); The complete truth about the life and death of Kurt Cobain (reading, Albany); Sunplay (reading, ET Berlin); Fireface, Pitbull, Shopping & Fucking, Like Skinnydipping (Gilded Balloon Studio Ensemble-founder and director 2001-2003)

AS ASSISTANT DIRECTOR: F.I.N.D. Festival 2006/2008, Platonov (Schaubühne, Berlin); Woyzeck (Gate); The Last Waltz Season (Arcola), La Sonnambula (Holland Park Opera).

INTERNATIONAL PLAYWRIGHTS AT THE ROYAL COURT

Since 1992 the Royal Court has placed a renewed emphasis on the development of international work and a creative dialogue now exists with theatre practitioners all over the world including Brazil, Cuba, France, Germany, India, Mexico, Nigeria, Palestine, Romania, Russia, Spain and Syria, and with writers from seven countries from the Near East and North Africa region. All of these development projects are supported by the Genesis Foundation and the British Council.

The Royal Court has produced new International plays through this programme since 1997, most recently *Bliss* by Olivier Choinière, translated by Caryl Churchill. In 2007, the Royal Court presented a season of five new international plays – *The Ugly One* by Marius von Mayenburg (Germany), *Kebab* by Gianina Carbunariu (Romania), *Free Outgoing* by Anupama Chandrasekhar (India), and a double bill of *The Good Family* by Joakim Prininen (Sweden) and *The Khomenko Family Chronicles* by Natalia Vorozhbit (Ukraine). Other recent work includes *On Insomnia* and *Midnight* by Edgar Chías (Mexico), *My Name is Rachel Corrie*, edited from the writings of Rachel Corrie by Alan Rickman and Katharine Viner, *Way to Heaven* by Juan Mayorga (Spain), *Amid the Clouds* by Amir Reza Koohestani (Iran), *At the Table* and *Almost Nothing* by Marcos Barbosa (Brazil), *Plasticine*, *Black Milk* and *Ladybird* by Vassily Sigarev (Russia), and *Terrorism* and *Playing the Victim* by the Presnyakov Brothers (Russia).

New German Playwrights at the Royal Court

The Royal Court began an exchange with new German playwrights in 1993 with the support of the Goethe-Institut, London. In 1994 a formal exchange continued between writers in both countries through a partnership with the Baracke of the Deutsches Theater, Berlin which later became a collaboration with the Schaubühne, Berlin.

Over the last 15 years, dozens of plays have been translated and produced as part of this long-term collaboration which has had a great impact on new writing in both countries. New German plays produced in translation at the Royal Court include: *Waiting Room Germany* (Klaus Pohl, 1995); *Strangers House* (Dea Loher, 1997); *Mr Kolpert* (David Gieselmann, 2000); *Fireface* (Marius von Mayenburg, 2000); *Push Up* (Roland Schimmelpfennig, 2002); *The Woman Before* (Roland Schimmelpfennig, 2005) and *The Ugly One* (Marius von Mayenburg, 2007 & 2008) and *The Stone* (Marius von Mayenburg, 2009). All of this work has been supported by the Genesis Foundation and the Goethe-Institut.

The Genesis Foundation supports the Royal Court's International Playwrights Programme. To find and develop the next generation of professional playwrights, Genesis funds workshops in diverse countries as well as residencies at the Royal Court. The Foundation's involvement extends to productions and rehearsed readings. Genesis helps the Royal Court offer a springboard for young writers to greater public and critical attention. For more information, please visit www.genesisfoundation.org.uk

OVER THERE is presented as part of International Playwrights, A Genesis Project, and produced by the Royal Court's International Department:

Associate Director **Elyse Dodgson**
International Administrator **Chris James**
International Assistant **William Drew**

ALMEIDA
THEATRE

19 March – 9 May 2009
European Premiere

Parlour Song
By Jez Butterworth

Cast:

Amanda Drew
Toby Jones
Andrew Lincoln

Director Ian Rickson
Design Jeremy Herbert
Lighting Peter Mumford
Music Stephen Warbeck

Tickets £6 - £29.50
No booking fee

Box Office **020 7359 4404**
Book and join e-list at
www.almeida.co.uk

Production Sponsor: Aspen Re
Principal Sponsor: Coutts & Co

ROYAL COURT

Wallace Shawn Season

2 April – 2 May

the fever
By Wallace Shawn

The Fever turns the heat up on individual responsibility and the balance of power. **Clare Higgins** delivers Shawn's seminal play.

Tickets £12 £18 £25
020 7565 5000
www.royalcourttheatre.com

THE ENGLISH STAGE COMPANY
AT THE ROYAL COURT

'For me the theatre is really a religion or way of life. You must decide what you feel the world is about and what you want to say about it, so that everything in the theatre you work in is saying the same thing ... A theatre must have a recognisable attitude. It will have one, whether you like it or not.'

George Devine, first artistic director of the English Stage Company: notes for an unwritten book.

photo: Stephen Cummiskey

As Britain's leading national company dedicated to new work, the Royal Court Theatre produces new plays of the highest quality, working with writers from all backgrounds, and addressing the problems and possibilities of our time.

"The Royal Court has been at the centre of British cultural life for the past 50 years, an engine room for new writing and constantly transforming the theatrical culture." Stephen Daldry

Since its foundation in 1956, the Royal Court has presented premieres by almost every leading contemporary British playwright, from John Osborne's *Look Back in Anger* to Caryl Churchill's *A Number* and Tom Stoppard's *Rock 'n' Roll*. Just some of the other writers to have chosen the Royal Court to premiere their work include Edward Albee, John Arden, Richard Bean, Samuel Beckett, Edward Bond, Jez Butterworth, Martin Crimp, Ariel Dorfman, Christopher Hampton, David Hare, Eugène Ionesco, Ann Jellicoe, Terry Johnson, Sarah Kane, David Mamet, Martin McDonagh, Conor McPherson, Joe Penhall, Mark Ravenhill, Simon Stephens, Wole Soyinka, Polly Stenham, David Storey, Debbie Tucker Green, Arnold Wesker and Roy Williams.

"It is risky to miss a production there." Financial Times

In addition to its full-scale productions, the Royal Court also facilitates international work at a grass roots level, developing exchanges which bring young writers to Britain and sending British writers, actors and directors to work with artists around the world. The research and play development arm of the Royal Court Theatre, The Studio, finds the most exciting and diverse range of new voices in the UK. The Studio runs playwriting groups including the Young Writers Programme, Critical Mass for black, Asian and minority ethnic writers and the bi-annual Young Writers Festival For further information, go to www.royalcourttheatre.com/ywp

"Yes, the Royal Court is on a roll. Yes, Dominic Cooke has just the genius and kick that this venue needs... It's fist-bitingly exciting." Independent

PROGRAMME SUPPORTERS

The Royal Court (English Stage Company Ltd) receives its principal funding from Arts Council England, London. It is also supported financially by a wide range of private companies, charitable and public bodies, and earns the remainder of its income from the box office and its own trading activities.

The Genesis Foundation supports the Royal Court's work with International Playwrights.

The Jerwood Charitable Foundation supports new plays by new playwrights through the Jerwood New Playwrights series.

The Artistic Director's Chair is supported by a lead grant from The Peter Jay Sharp Foundation, contributing to the activities of the Artistic Director's office. Over the past ten years the BBC has supported the Gerald Chapman Fund for directors.

ROYAL COURT DEVELOPMENT ADVOCATES
John Ayton
Elizabeth Bandeen
Anthony Burton
Sindy Caplan
Cas Donald
Allie Esiri
Celeste Fenichel
Stephen Marquardt
Emma Marsh (Vice Chair)
Mark Robinson
William Russell (Chair)
David Winterfeldt

PUBLIC FUNDING
Arts Council England, London
British Council

CHARITABLE DONATIONS
American Friends of the Royal Court Theatre
Anthony Burton
Gerald Chapman Fund
The Sidney & Elizabeth Corob Charitable Trust
Cowley Charitable Trust
Credit Suisse First Boston Foundation *
The Edmond de Rothschild Foundation*
Do Well Foundation Ltd*
The D'Oyly Carte Charitable Trust
Esmée Fairbairn Foundation
The Edwin Fox Foundation
Francis Finlay*
Frederick Loewe Foundation *
Genesis Foundation
Haberdashers' Company
Jerwood Charitable Foundation
John Thaw Foundation
Kudos Film and Televisoin
Lynn Foundation
John Lyon's Charity
The Laura Pels Foundation*
The Martin Bowley Charitable Trust
The Patchwork Charitable Foundation*
Paul Hamlyn FoundationQuercus Charitable Trust
Jerome Robbins Foundation*
Rose Foundation
The Rosenkranz Foundation*
The Peter Jay Sharp Foundation*
Sobell Foundation

CORPORATE SUPPORTERS & SPONSORS
BBC
Hugo Boss
Links of London

BUSINESS BENEFACTORS & MEMBERS
Grey London
Lazard
Merrill Lynch
Vanity Fair

INDIVIDUAL SUPPORTERS

ICE-BREAKERS
Act IV
Anonymous
Ossi & Paul Burger
Mrs Helena Butler
Cynthia Corbett
Shantelle David
Charlotte & Nick Fraser
Mark & Rebecca Goldbart
Linda Grosse
Mr & Mrs Tim Harvey-Samuel
The David Hyman Charitable Trust
David Lanch
Colette & Peter Levy
Watcyn Lewis
David Marks
Nicola McFarland
Janet & Michael Orr
Pauline Pinder
Mr & Mrs William Poeton
The Really Useful Group
Lois Sieff OBE
Gail Steele
Nick & Louise Steidl

GROUND-BREAKERS
Anonymous
Moira Andreae
Jane Attias*
Elizabeth & Adam Bandeen
Philip Blackwell
Mrs D H Brett
Sindy & Jonathan Caplan
Mr & Mrs Gavin Casey
Carole & Neville Conrad
Clyde Cooper
Andrew & Amanda Cryer
Robyn M Durie
Hugo Eddis
Mrs Margaret Exley CBE
Robert & Sarah Fairbairn
Celeste & Peter Fenichel
Andrew & Jane Fenwick
Ginny Finegold
Wendy Fisher
Hugh & Henri Fitzwilliam-Lay
Joachim Fleury
John Garfield
Lydia & Manfred Gorvy
Richard & Marcia Grand*
Reade and Elizabeth Griffith
Nick & Catherine Hanbury-Williams
Sam & Caroline Haubold
Mr & Mrs J Hewett
Nicholas Josefowitz
David P Kaskel & Christopher A Teano
Peter & Maria Kellner*
Mrs Joan Kingsley & Mr Philip Kingsley
Mr & Mrs Pawel Kisielewski
Varian Ayers & Gary Knisely
Rosemary Leith
Kathryn Ludlow
Emma Marsh
Barbara Minto
Gavin & Ann Neath
William Plapinger & Cassie Murray*
Mark Robinson
Paul & Jill Ruddock
William & Hilary Russell
Jenny Sheridan
Anthony Simpson & Susan Boster
Brian Smith
Carl & Martha Tack
Katherine & Michael Yates

BOUNDARY-BREAKERS
John and Annoushka Ayton
Katie Bradford
Tim Fosberry
Edna & Peter Goldstein
Sue & Don Guiney
Rosanna Laurence
The David & Elaine Potter Charitable Foundation

MOVER-SHAKERS
Anonymous
Dianne & Michael Bienes*
Lois Cox
Cas & Philip Donald
Duncan Matthews QC
Ian & Carol Sellars
Jan & Michael Topham

HISTORY-MAKERS
Jack & Linda Keenan*
Miles Morland

MAJOR DONORS
Daniel & Joanna Friel
Deborah & Stephen Marquardt
Lady Sainsbury of Turville
NoraLee & Jon Sedmak*

*Supporters of the American Friends of the Royal Cour

FOR THE ROYAL COURT

Royal Court Theatre, Sloane Square, London SW1W 8AS
Tel: 020 7565 5050 Fax: 020 7565 5001
info@royalcourttheatre.com, www.royalcourttheatre.com

Artistic Director **Dominic Cooke**
Associate Directors **Ramin Gray***, **Jeremy Herrin**, **Sacha Wares**+
Artistic Associate **Emily McLaughlin**
Associate Producer **Diane Borger**
Diversity Associate **Ola Animashawun***
Education Associate **Lynne Gagliano***
Trainee Director (ITV Scheme) **Natalie Ibu**‡
PA to the Artistic Director **Victoria Reilly**

Literary Manager **Ruth Little**
Literary Associate **Terry Johnson***
Senior Reader **Nicola Wass****
Pearson Playwright **Daniel Jackson**†
Literary Assistant **Marcelo Dos Santos**

Associate Director International **Elyse Dodgson**
International Administrator **Chris James**
International Assistant **William Drew**

Studio Administrator **Clare McQuillan**
Studio Intern **Lara Hickey**
Writers' Tutor **Leo Butler**

Casting Director **Amy Ball**
Casting Assistant **Lotte Hines**

Head of Production **Paul Handley**
JTU Production Managers **Sue Bird, Tariq Rifaat**
Production Administrator **Sarah Davies**
Head of Lighting **Matt Drury**
Lighting Deputy **Nicki Brown**
Lighting Board Operator **Tom Lightbody**
Lighting Assistants **Stephen Andrews, Katie Pitt**
Head of Stage **Steven Stickler**
Stage Deputy **Duncan Russell**
Stage Chargehand **Lee Crimmen**
Chargehand Carpenter **Richard Martin**
Head of Sound **Ian Dickinson**
Sound Deputy **David McSeveney**
Head of Costume **Iona Kenrick**
Costume Deputy **Jackie Orton**
Wardrobe Assistant **Pam Anson**
Sound Operator **Alex Caplen**

Executive Director **Kate Horton**
Head of Finance and Administration **Helen Perryer**
Planning Administrator **Davina Shah**
Senior Finance and Administration Officer **Martin Wheeler**
Finance Officer **Rachel Harrison***
Finance and Administration Assistant **Tessa Rivers**
Interim PA to the Executive Director **Frances Marden**

Head of Communications **Kym Bartlett**
Marketing Manager **Becky Wootton**
Press & Public Affairs Officer **Stephen Pidcock**
Audience Development Officer **Gemma Frayne**
Communications Interns **Ruth Hawkins, Stephanie Hui**
Sales Manager **Kevin West**
Deputy Sales Manager **Daniel Alicandro**
Box Office Sales Assistants **Ed Fortes, Shane Hough, Ciara O'Toole**

Senior Development Manager **Hannah Clifford**
Corporate Partnerships Manager **Sarah Drake***
Development Officer **Lucy James**
Development Assistant **Penny Saward**

Theatre Manager **Bobbie Stokes**
Front of House Manager **Claire Simpson**
Deputy Theatre Manager **Daniel O'Neill**
Café Bar Managers **Paul Carstairs, Katy Mudge**
Head Chef **Stuart Jenkyn**
Bookshop Manager **Simon David**
Assistant Bookshop Manager **Edin Suljic***
Bookshop Assistant **Emily Lucienne**
Building Maintenance Administrator **Jon Hunter**
Stage Door/Reception **Simon David***, **Paul Lovegrove, Tyrone Lucas**

Thanks to all of our box office assistants, ushers and bar staff.

+ Sacha Wares' post is supported by the BBC through the Gerald Chapman Fund.
** The post of Senior Reader is supported by NoraLee and Jon Sedmak through the American Friends of the Royal Court Theatre.
‡ The post of Trainee Director is supported by ITV under the ITV Theatre Director Scheme.

† This theatre has the support of the Pearson Playwrights' scheme, sponsored by the Peggy Ramsay Foundation.

* Part-time.

ENGLISH STAGE COMPANY

Vice President
Dame Joan Plowright CBE

Honorary Council
Sir Richard Eyre CBE
Alan Grieve CBE
Martin Paisner CBE

Council
Chairman **Anthony Burton**
Vice Chairman **Graham Devlin**

Members
Jennette Arnold
Judy Daish
Sir David Green KCMG
Joyce Hytner OBE
Stephen Jeffreys
Wasfi Kani OBE
Phyllida Lloyd
James Midgley
Sophie Okonedo
Alan Rickman
Anita Scott
Katharine Viner
Stewart Wood

Over There

for Fundi, with love

Characters

Karl
Franz

Punctuation

When the text is in bold type **like this** the characters are speaking at the same time.

When the text is in parentheses (like this) the characters are speaking to an offstage character.

Punctuation like this

. . .

means the scene has skipped forward a few minutes.

When you see this / it is the cue for the next person to speak, creating overlapping dialogue.

Thanks

Thank you to all those in Berlin I interviewed while researching the play: Irma Zwernemann, Gertraud Tietz, Nico Felden, Lilly Henze, Dr Peter Becker, Sabine Rätsch, Liselotte Kubitza, Ludwig Bodemann, Richard Graf zu Eulenburg.

The interviews were organised by Nicole Nikutowski.

Thanks to Dominic, Diane, Ramin and Ruth at the Royal Court, and Thomas, Tobias, Marius, Maja and Jens at the Schaubühne.

Prologue

California. The present.

Carly Where you from?

Franz Germany.

Carly In Europe? No way.

Franz Germany in Europe. Yes.

Carly My family's Polish. Gdansk. I'll go visit. One day. When I'm an old lady. You? Bet you one day you're gonna want to –

Franz No. Never. Germany's dead. I'm gonna stay right here in California until the day I die.

Carly . . . You wanna come home with me? Most days when the diner's shut I sit down and roll myself a joint and let go. You want to let go with me?

Franz Sure. That'd be good.

Carly Here, you roll for me while I finish off. I like your face. We'll have beers, music, joint and then we'll . . . well, then we'll see.

Franz Let's see.

Carly Hi. I'm Carly.

Franz Oh.

Carly Now you're supposed to say 'That's a pretty name'.

Franz Okay. That's a **pretty name**.

Carly There. That wasn't so difficult was it?

One

East Berlin, 1986.

a.

Franz I'm sorry. There was a woman in front of me. There was something wrong. They held her for hours. She got so upset and she was crying and screaming and swearing and I had to wait and it was . . . I'm sorry.

Karl Hello Franzl.

Franz Hello Karli.

Karl Did you bring the chocolate?

Franz Let's go for a **beer**.

b.

Karl And I would turn the TV aerial and I sometimes I thought I saw you in the programmes – like you were winning a car or something or on the news you'd be like a terrorist.

Franz A terrorist. Hah! Great.

Karl Or you'd be an actor in a soap opera only of course it wasn't ever you. And then Papa would come back and he would be: What the fuck do you think you're doing **turning the aerial West. We don't turn the aerial West in this house. Turn it right back again** . . . How did you do that?

Franz Do what?

Karl Do that. Yes. That. That's it. That.

Franz Oh my . . . That's weird, that's strange. I didn't plan it. It just . . .

Karl Happened? Like that?

Franz Happened. **Like that.** Yes. There have been times . . . all these years when you weren't there when I saw things, felt things that I thought were your stuff but I didn't think hah! We'd **say the same things at the same time**. Hah! I liked it. I know so much about you.

c.

Franz It was very hot. It was summer. Aug— No, early **September**. Because it felt like you were in . . . it was a . . . it was . . . there was a lake . . . a forest . . . huge trees . . . the air was so clear . . . **summer camp**?

Karl Young Pioneers.

Franz I saw that place so clear, like I was there. And you were watching her for a week. I felt it like this – mmm – **tension**.

Karl Yes.

Franz In my stomach for a week I could feel it like you were **watching** her all the time but not **talking**.

Karl Exactly **yes** exactly.

Franz But then finally you . . . late . . . and she led you down this it was a corridor something –

Karl It was a doorway. Doorway of the shower house.

Franz There was **rain**. Really heavy.

Karl Really **heavy**.

Franz And you got mud on your knees your belly your arse

Karl Hah! I did. **Mud up my arse.**

Franz And you were **really** you know, droopy **because** but finally she you know **worked** you into –

Karl Took time –

Franz Worked you and then but once you'd actually **entered** her finally then –

Karl It was my first time.

Franz When you came . . . I came.

Karl . . . Really?

Franz Yes. Came. Which was so . . . I was watching TV with Mama and all this was so clear like I felt myself going into her and when you **came I came**.

Karl That's brilliant.

Franz Sitting there with Mama with jizz in my pants. What do you know about me?

d.

Karl And you would say to Mama: Everything is wrong with our world. **This decadent this bloated this smug and yes I would kidnap a child I would blow up a banker I would tear the facade of this sham world away.**

Franz Hah! I did. I was a fucking pain.

Karl And Mama would cry and: **So what you rather? Would you rather be over there?** And you'd say: **Well maybe I would.**

Franz I was a little shit. You know too much about me.

. . .

Karl And then in a bar she told you that she was having your child.

Franz You know about that?

Karl You only met her two months ago at the party with the smell of marijuana. That's the first time I felt her in your –

Franz That was the first time. It was. You know everything.

Karl And now she's **pregnant**. Yes? And in that bar you really, it really felt like you were going to hit her, strike her in the jaw. I'm twenty-two you bitch twenty-two and I don't want to be a **father** and why didn't – use **something** – I just assumed you were going to – because there's no way I – only thought I'd see you **a few weeks** and now . . .

Franz   But I didn't.

Karl   I know.

Franz   I would never hit a . . . You know that?

Karl   Of course not. You held her and said I **love** you.

Franz   I did. Yes. I love you.

e.

Franz   This was a good idea. When shall we do it again? How about next month?

Karl   Next month would be great.

Franz   Let's say four weeks today . . . Of course I'll have to check the baby coming and everything I . . .

Karl   Of course you will, of course. Will you see Mama?

Franz   Tomorrow.

Karl   Will you tell Mama that Karli says hello?

Franz   Listen I actually I . . . Well I actually I . . . **didn't tell Mama that we were meeting**. I'm sorry.

Karl   I see.

Franz   She wouldn't have wanted . . . she wouldn't want me to come over here . . . she doesn't think anyone should come over, she . . . it's . . . it's just her strange . . . she still hates everything to do with over here.

Karl   Of course. But her son –

Franz   She's not very well. The doctor there's been tests. She –

Karl   What do they – ?

Franz   Cancer. Mama has cancer so –

Karl   I see.

Franz Which could be totally – if we hit it aggressively we may . . .

Karl I want to see her.

Franz I'm sure.

Karl Twenty years and I still smell her, I still –

Franz I have to go. The queue at the checkpoint's long.

Karl Let's swap passports.

Franz What?

Karl You take mine. You stay East. Just a few days. I'll take yours. I'll see Mama.

Franz Impossible.

Karl Nobody will know. A few days I'll get a visa back here you can go home.

Franz I don't want to do that.

Karl We're twins. You like that. We can pass for each other. I'll give you the keys to my apartment. It's not so bad over here. It'll be an adventure. Step through the mirror. Welcome to the East.

Franz No.

Karl No?

Franz I've got a job, a girlfriend, there's –

Karl She's my mother too, my mother is dying and you won't even let me –

Franz She'll get she might get better she –

Karl It's my right to step through that wall.

Franz You stayed here with Papa. You don't know her any more.

Karl A child always knows its mother.

Franz I'm sorry maybe it's me I'm a coward what if you went over there and didn't come back? If I was stuck over here. I couldn't stand that.

Karl Why did you come here?

Franz You're my brother. It was natural.

Karl Track me down? Write the letters? An adventure? Take a look? 'What if it had been me? Just imagine. Just imagine if Mama had left me behind. What if – oh horrible – if I had to live in the East. Just one day and back to my fat girlfriend and my fat life.'

Franz I've got a kid on the way. I wanted to –

Karl Don't miss the checkpoint Franz. Back to the West.

Franz I'll write on Monday.

Karl You don't want to get stuck over here do you?

Franz Shall I write?

Karl I don't think so.

Two

West Berlin, 1988.

a.

Franz How did you get here?

Karl I got a travel pass.

Franz Why didn't you tell me?

Karl I heard from Ursula that Mama was really bad. I got a letter from the hospital. Ursula helped me. And so I got a travel pass. How's Mama?

Franz You should have told me you wanted to come over here. I would have helped you.

Karl Are you sure about that?

Franz Of course I would.

Karl I'm not sure I like it over here. It's flashy, loud. We have better hospitals in the East.

Franz They've looked after Mama very well here.

Karl She would have got much better care back home.

Franz This is our home.

Karl Where's her ward?

Franz Listen –

Karl You're not going to stop me seeing her now I've come over here?

Franz She's – . . . Mama died an hour ago. At three thirty more or less she . . . it was really such a combination of things the cancer was so widely but in the end it was her heart that couldn't that's what they're going to put on the death certificate heart failure it was her heart.

Karl Oh.

Franz I was with her when she . . .

Karl Oh. Wouldn't it have been good don't you think if she could have had both her twins with her at the moment of death? She would have got better care at home. In our hospitals we –

Franz Communism kills cancer? Well, clever communism.

Karl She shouldn't have left. This would never have happened if she stayed at home.

Franz She had a good life. It was a dignified death. I was with her.

Karl I should have been there. Did she mention me? You know. At the end.

Franz They fill you with morphine. She was in a dream.

Karl Did she say my name?

Franz I don't – She mumbled. Sounds. Nothing I understood.

Karl I don't like it here. The West is strange. I'm going home.

Franz I thought about you. I was holding her hand. Three o'clock or so. And I thought: I bet he knows this. Bet he's feeling this as I'm . . .

Karl Well. No. Not a fucking thing.

Franz I thought my twin would –

Karl You're a very sentimental person aren't you?

Franz Let's go back to mine. I'll show you my place. I'd like to show you where I live. Will you come? I'll feed you.

Karl I've only got a few hours.

Franz Please.

b.

Franz I'd like to see Papa.

Karl That's not possible.

Franz If I get a day pass, come East, we could take him for a meal. I'll pay. Will you tell him Mama died?

Karl He doesn't like me to talk about her. He says it was her choice to come West. And he hated her. And she brought you up over here and so – he says – he couldn't bear to see you.

Franz Still. I'd like to see him.

Karl It's never going to happen. Papa is still totally he is still totally our workers' democracy our workers' democracy the finest country in the world. He says, he does – I'm sorry – say you're not his son any more.

Franz How was the chicken?

Karl Good. I say open your eye Papa surely you can see –

Franz There's some more.

Karl Surely you can see –

Franz Would you like some more chicken? A sausage?

Karl But he's still – this is the best way of life.

Franz He's a man of his time.

Karl Things are changing. But he hates that. He won't survive without communism.

Franz Life over here isn't so great. I don't like my job. My relationship's lousy. I split up with the mother of my child. At first it was argue fuck argue fuck. Now it's just argue argue still no fuck argue. I see my boy five days a month.

Karl That's how it is with relationships. Everything's temporary.

Franz I'd like you to meet him sometime. Uncle Karl.

Two 13

Karl Then you'll have to bring him East won't you?

Franz If I opened some wine would you drink it with me?

Karl Of course I would.

Franz *goes to fetch wine.* **Karl** *sees videos.*

Karl What's this say? *Wixn pussi.* What does that mean? *Wixn pussi?*

Franz What? Oh. *Vixen Pussies.*

Karl *Wixen?*

Franz A vixen in English is like . . . I don't know actually it's . . . I don't know what a vixen is.

Karl This is quite a collection.

Franz I'm a lonely man. Sometimes I need you know release.

Karl Let's watch one. This one. You can translate the dialogue.

Franz There's hardly any –

Karl But still – you translate the dialogue.

Franz If you like.

He plays the video.

I'm a good country girl. She's saying that her . . . that she lives in this cabin in the forest by the lake because she's and . . . mmm . . . she wants to . . . yes . . . and has he got a . . . a . . . it's a delivery for her . . . yes . . . has he got a delivery for her . . . and she . . . she wants to erm . . . yes . . . she'd like to give him something for his trouble . . . would he like to come inside? But come inside she says it in such a way that you see come inside you see come inside so . . .

Karl It's not working. I keep thinking about all that cancer inside Mama.

Franz So do I.

c.

Franz Can you get over here again?

Karl It was only cos of Mama. Otherwise I wouldn't get the papers so I . . .

Franz I could come over to you. Next month. I'll bring my boy.

Karl Papa doesn't want me to see you.

Franz But still –

Karl I think it's best if I do what he says. You've got a nice place. That was a great meal. I bet you're a good father. Goodbye.

Three

West Berlin, 1989.

a.

Karl The wall's falling.

Franz I know.

Karl You can just – ha – you can just walk through the –

Franz I know and that's –

Karl I just walked through the – I just walked through the fuck I just walked through the fuck and there wasn't a fucker fucking stop me fucking –

Franz Great.

Karl I want here Franzl. Tonight. The wall fell and I thought: What do I do? Where do I go? What do I want? And I realised: I wanted to be – you here tonight. I wanted. Karli Franzl.

Franz I know. I know that because I did actually – yes – feel your feeling as you're standing there and they're pulling you **over the wall** and the crowd are **tearing at the bricks** I did actually see that through your eyes which was amazing.

Karl The wall's down the wall's down the wall's down the wall's down just cracked open the possibilities the centuries of the weight of the everything still slow static no nothing and you don't think it's ever and suddenly splits and fast the people claiming this is ours burn out the old cut it and we are the free now the oh the possibilities we can be anything I can be anything I. Who am I now? Who am I? I. Can be anything. Free choose I liberate I . . .

Franz We watched it on the television. I felt so proud.

Karl You're my brother. I was over there. You were over here. No more. Here. There. We're . . . everywhere. No. We're both here. I love you.

Franz And I do love you – yes – I love you too.

Karl Out on the street come on out on the fucking come.

Franz I can't I.

Karl Dance.

Franz I can't no I – the boy's here. I've got my boy here.

Karl Then bring your –

Franz No. He's asleep now. I just got him off to –

Karl Okay. Could I look at him? Take a little look. Does he look like you?

Franz Go on. Quietly. Take a quiet look.

Karl *looks at the boy.*

Karl He does. He's got your nose. Hah! He's got my nose.

Franz We watched it together on the television. I don't think he really understood. But I did my best. I wanted him to understand. I was trying to teach him what this meant but I don't think he understood. But still. I sat him there with the screen because when History is . . .

Karl I want some more beer.

Franz I don't have any more beer. Maybe a bit of . . .

Karl Vodka would be great.

Franz Are you staying tonight?

Karl I don't know. Am I ?

Franz Come on. Special night. No more wall. In my **bed**. Head to toe.

Karl Well – yes – one night – why not yes? **In the bed. Head to toe. Karli and Franzl in the bed head to toe just like old times. Head to toe.**

b.

Karl And we both had to be at a party or a fair or something . . . I don't know, something . . . and Mama got us both dressed up identically . . . she took us to the shop and she . . . trouser, shirt, tie . . . shoes . . . all of it totally . . . but you wouldn't sit still . . . the photographer was this fat old – with big patches of sweat under both arms . . . you kept on getting up and running around . . . and Mama actually cried, she actually cried – the frustration . . . because she'd gone to all this trouble expense with the little outfits but she couldn't get you to sit and the photographer was getting really angry about his time and the money and in the end he went away and Mama was so cross because she didn't get her photo. Do you remember that? Do you?

Franz I've forgotten that.

c.

Franz And we're inside the car in the dark holding on to each other really tight and we're both bleeding the windscreen had – so I suppose there's a lot of blood and Mama is calling out to us 'Are you all right boys? Can you hear me? The emergency services are going to cut you out.' But none of us answered her. 'Boys are you there are you there are you there?'

Karl It didn't happen.

Franz Funny cos I can see it as clear as –

Karl No.

Franz It really is so –

Karl Just a bad dream.

Franz So many years I thought . . .

Karl Nothing like that ever happened. You were always having nightmares.

18   Over There

d.

Karl   I've been to the shops. And I bought a lot of shit. You have such a lot of shit in the shops. I love that. Totally unnecessary shit. So I went a bit – I went shopping crazy. You live in colour over here. We always lived in black and white. Look at this. You have to take a look at my shit. Good morning.

Franz   Good morning.

Karl   I've been shopping. You're looking smart.

Franz   I don't really like it.

Karl   It's a good suit.

Franz   It's a meeting of the sales team. We all have to drive out to this hotel near the airport and listen to all these presentations and . . . everybody has to look . . . this team fly in from head office . . . we're all sitting there in these suits . . . And they tell us about the way forward . . . motivation . . . it's incredibly boring.

Karl   You should wear that more often.

Franz   I'd like to burn the fucking thing. I've got two more just the same. I hate buying suits so . . . Try one on if you like.

Karl   I ought to go back.

Franz   Stay a bit longer. I'm taking the boy to his mother's tonight. I'm a free man.

Karl   All right then. I will.

e.

Franz   Fucking boring. The developing market to the East. For eight fucking hours. The developing market to the East. The overhead projector broke down a few times. That was the best bit. The developing market to the East.

Karl *is in* **Franz**'s *suit*

Three 19

Karl 'Fucking boring. The developing market to the East. For eight fucking hours. The developing market to the East. The overhead projector broke down a few times. That was the best bit. The developing market to the East.'

Franz Woo!

Karl 'I hate suits. I hate buying suits. So it was easier . . . ' What do you think?

Franz Brilliant.

Karl Look, come on, stand here. If you stand there and . . .

Franz Brilliant that's brilliant. It's a mirror. Ha ha. That is fucking great. I love that. I fucking love that, it's a mirror.

Karl You want **a beer, a steak and a shag.** And so do I **a beer, a steak and a shag**. So let's

Franz Keep

Karl The

Franz Suits

Karl On

Franz And

Karl Get

Franz A

Karl Beer

Franz A

Karl Steak

Franz And

Karl A

Franz Shag.

f.

Karl/Franz How much you had? Woah, must be gone. You must have since lunchtime. Two? I don't think. Two? In your dreams. In your fucking. What so there's another? I don't see. There's only me. There's only special unique wonderful you better believe it.

. . .

Reckon you could take it twice? Hungry enough? Big enough? You wide? You wet? Double the? In your fucking.

. . .

Open wide the twins are coming inside.

g.

Franz You can keep the suit.

Karl No that's okay.

Franz Go on you keep it it's not a –

Karl That's okay it's your suit. I don't want to take –

Franz Well all right then.

Karl I've really enjoyed this.

Franz I've loved it. We can travel backwards and forwards when we like now can't we?

Karl I'll try. But there's still Papa to look after so I . . .

Franz Of course. And I've got the boy.

Karl Of course.

Franz For the boy I really it's really important that I – I have to give all my focus to the boy –

Karl Of course you do. And Papa's not easy. Sometimes it's so bad I have to wipe the shit off his arse.

Franz I'd really like you to keep the suit.

Karl Well okay.

Franz You look really great in the – keep the –

Karl I'll have to put it in a drawer. I don't want Papa to see this.

Four

West Berlin, 1990.

a.

Karl He just gave up. He didn't want to live any longer. He believed in that farmers and workers, a democracy of – totally and utterly. Impossible to imagine. But there we go. That was actually his reason for living that was his totally –

Franz I wish I could have seen him just one last –

Karl I don't think he would have –

Franz But he could have been persuaded towards the end surely he could have –

Karl I really don't think he could have.

Franz Well. Goodbye Papa.

Karl Ashes to ashes dust to dust.

Franz Look at us. **We're orphans.**

Karl There's your boy.

Franz Yes. Life goes on.

b.

Karl Can I read him a story?

Franz Yes, why not? What story?

Karl Maybe *The Town Band*?

Franz Oh yes he loves that one. Do the donkey. Eeee-hore.

Karl Eeee-hore okay.

Franz I'll cook the meat. Listen. I think you should change.

Karl Yes?

Franz I think you should change out of the suit before you read the story.

Karl It's fine.

Franz No really – I don't want you to read him the story when you're wearing my suit.

Karl It doesn't bother him.

Franz You've done it before?

Karl Quite a few times. When you were out. He asks me to put on the suit.

Franz I'd rather you didn't.

Karl But if he likes it –

Franz I'm his father. It's my decision. It's my responsibility to decide what's best for him.

Karl But he told me he wants me to.

Franz It's too confusing. He's just forming . . . shaping . . . he's still trying to figure out the world . . . and I just think if there's two of us –

Karl You're being ridiculous.

Franz Maybe I am. But still –

Karl It's silly.

Franz But I just feel – on some level – two of us – because he associates the suit with me – two of us will traumatise him. You see?

Karl He knows. He likes it. It's a game.

Franz Yes but –

Karl Ask him. Go on. Surely he's allowed – surely you can . . . a democratic choice?

Franz (*Is oncle hastory bid washes the bact tread, bit, as for it learning une of me complarts, which doos nit concert my rally retarding he ist huppy. Whim the gity dolume in sour the comfart it neads, being?*)

Franz He says yes it's fine read him the story in the suit.

Karl Were you talking to him in English?

Franz Yes that's right. In English.

Karl Why did you do that?

Franz It's just something we do from time to time.

Karl What did you say to him?

Franz Nothing much. Go on. He's waiting for you. Read him the story. In German. I'll prepare the meat.

. . .

Karl (Eee-hore. Eee-hore. Woof woof woof woof wooof meee-ow meeee-ow meee-ow cock a doodle doo cock a doodle doo they chased the robber down the road and now the house is all theirs.)

Franz *cuts himself chopping the meat.*

. . .

Karl He's becoming more and more like you.

Franz I don't notice it.

Karl Oh yes. Look at that –

Franz What?

Karl The way you do that – rub your nose like that he does that.

Franz I hadn't spotted that.

Karl Oh yes and that hair thing.

Franz What hair thing?

Karl You pull at your hair.

Franz Do I?

Karl Yes – like this – see? – you do it like this.

Franz Really? Like this?

Karl Yes. And he does that too. And he says chicken just the same as you and just the same as me. Chicken. We all of us say chicken just the same.

Franz Do we? **Chicken. Chicken. Chicken.**

Karl You see exactly yes.

Franz I suppose that's right.

Karl He's turning out to be just like you.

Franz I don't want that.

Karl But it's happening.

Franz I want him to be himself. I want him to be special unique one of a kind.

Karl He's happy.

Franz He doesn't want to be like me. I'm a bit of a fuck- up.

Karl No you're not you're great.

Franz I can't sustain a relationship my job is boredom I am total fuck-up.

Karl He thinks you're amazing.

Franz He's better off being his own person.

Karl You've cut yourself. You're bleeding.

Franz It's nothing. See there all gone.

Karl Maybe I'll learn English. Then I can talk to him in English like you.

Franz Maybe you should. He'd enjoy that.

Karl I'll learn English. Will you help me?

Franz If you like.

c.

Franz *How much time have you have lived in California?*

Karl *Now I have . . . er . . .* **lived** *California since three years.*

Franz *What things do you appreciate the best living in California?*

Karl *Task that is the . . . er . . . sun but* **moreover** *the . . .* **buffet salad** *it . . .* **eats** *as well as as* **appreciate**.

Franz Good. Really good, Karli. More.

Karl *This is my favourite thing approximately living in California.*

Franz *You enjoy the sun?*

Karl *Yes I enjoy the sun. But I must be,* er, *must be* er, *must be* **much** *careful one. My skin is much right one so as to . . .* Er . . . **burns** *very easy in sunlight in California.* I want to stop now. I'm bored. I'm too old for school.

Franz *What will you drinking?* Come on. *What will you be drinking?*

Karl *It is too soon for the . . . ?* No. I don't want to do this.

Franz But English is the language of –

Karl Fuck English. I hate it. It sounds shit. Fuck their language.

Franz Our language –

Karl I don't want it.

Franz But you're doing well. We can move on to the new tape next month. I thought you wanted to speak to the boy in English. It really is – not just for him – for you – you're going to need English we all need English.

Karl He understands me well enough.

d.

Karl (*Them grundfithers tedided tot redain min the leask if you grundmithers, who it ginleg tot he wesernt. Thit, how ye arrited to he sin morder hodated theres toll ind to men brings mout. Blut tham is tompletest snow inish. We fo aret sood mogether dow.*)

Franz Was that Russian?

Karl Yes that's right Russian.

Franz Why were you talking to him in Russian?

Karl He likes it.

Franz But he doesn't understand Russian.

Karl He does now. A few words. I'm teaching him.

Franz I don't think you should.

Karl Just a few words.

Franz No but really – he's got enough to learn – the world is full of information to stuff into a child without –

Karl All right then I'll stop.

Franz It's just really I mean now after everything that's happened Russian is dead dying isn't it really?

Karl Well I suppose so.

Franz So really I wouldn't – with a child you have to look to the future and Russia isn't really – talk to him in German.

e.

Franz What the fuck did you think you were doing?

Karl It was a joke.

Franz I'm not laughing.

Karl Well maybe you should.

Franz If his mother gets to hear about this –

Karl She won't. I told him it was a secret game.

Franz You fucking idiot.

Karl He thought it was funny.

Franz I waited outside that nursery school for an hour.

Karl I'm sorry.

Franz You wait outside the school. Your kid doesn't come out. You feel scared.

Karl I know.

Franz And then somebody says: Oh I think somebody already took him away.

Karl I thought you'd guess.

Franz Well I didn't.

Karl See what we were up to.

Franz And they get hold of the teacher on the phone and she says: But his **father** took him. The same man who collects him every day. Yes, of course I'm sure. **I know what his father looks like.** You tricked her.

Karl No I didn't.

Franz You let her think that you were me.

Karl It was actually his idea. Your son –

Franz Don't blame the child.

Karl Your child said that this was the game that he wanted to play.

Franz That's not an excuse. You should have told him. **You should have told him we're not playing that game. Stop doing that. Don't copy. You should have told him that is an inappropriate game to play. Stop it. This is serious. You cunt. Stop fucking copying me. Enough.** Look, he's moving about now. He's **supposed to be asleep and you've woken him up**. I'll go to him.

Franz (*I wat annayed hat I was our uncle came to the scil and the pretends I to be and it would not have gone that it was a strong shing, to do and we to heally meave ballen in much a day you us ejaminer, thether meever again hadden.*)

Karl I understood what you said.

Franz No you didn't.

Karl I know what you're saying when you speak English.

Franz What did I say then? Go on.

Karl You . . .

Franz You're full of shit.

Karl 'One of the greatest challenges is to train the Eastern worker to initiate and to innovate. The Eastern education system rewarded obedience and conformity. In some ways this was not a bad thing. The Eastern worker was a good team member and was supportive of fellow workers.' How am I doing?

Franz Stop that.

Karl 'But the worker from the former East struggles with the idea of individual initiative, the ethos that says competition within the company can deliver a better product and deliver excellent service to the customer.'

Franz You've got all the words. But you're still –

Karl 'So what we're going to be doing in today's workshop is looking at some exercises, some games and some tests which line managers can use to train staff from the former East to more effectively operate within the company.'

Franz You're not me.

Karl I could pass for you. I fooled the teacher. I could lead one of your training days.

Franz You fooled the teacher. For a moment. She was tired, end of the day, hundreds of parents –

Karl I could drive to your office. Sit at your desk. Offer your training programme. And no one would tell.

Franz No. People can tell. Honestly. There are . . . it's a nice idea really funny idea but actually honestly people would tell.

Karl You're sure of that?

Franz I'm sure of that.

Karl Elena at the next desk to you had a baby three months ago. She shows the photos every lunchtime.

Franz How do you know that?

Karl Thomas likes to talk to you about football. His desk is situated near the coffee machine.

Franz Stop it now.

Karl And if you end up in the stationary cupboard the same time as Ulrike: watch out because her perfume is so strong it makes you feel giddy you have to go outside for a breath of fresh air where – chances are – you'll find Gunter having a cigarette.

Franz How do you know all these . . . ?

Karl I was there.

Franz Fuck.

Karl The day you called in sick. I went in. 'Yeah I was feeling bad first thing but actually I felt fine once I was properly awake so I'm here now.' Your top drawer is such a mess you really need to . . . look at this banana must have been – what – I should say at least a week old.

Franz You cunt.

Karl Isn't it great? Any time you don't want to, I'll do things. You commit a crime, I'll go to court. You get a cough, I'll go the doctor. You want to marry again I can go to church. You can send me anywhere, any time and I'll be you.

Franz I don't want to do that.

Karl It'll be great fun.

Franz Please I just I, it's probably really stupid it's probably but being me being unique being special being the only – being special somehow that's terribly import— stop it now – I really need to feel like I'm the only one – please no don't do that any more. Can we not – ? Can we stop? Can we stop doing the talking at the same time thing and the wearing the suit thing and can we stop all that now?

Karl If you like.

Franz I would like yes.

Karl I don't see what the problem –

Franz What do you want? My kid? My job? My life? Well you can't. Because they're mine okay all this is mine. So what I'd like you to – you have to find your – find your own life Karli. Which is – you know – I mean how long are you going to stay here? How long till . . . ? You need your own job kid wife you're – And I think actually I think I'd like you to take off the suit.

Karl Now?

Franz Yes now.

Karl Oh.

Franz Just to avoid any . . . confusion I think it's best if you . . .

Karl Right. I . . .

Franz Yes?

Karl I don't have any of my own clothes with me. I – I threw all the clothes I had away. I didn't like them. They looked too . . . East . . . so I . . .

Franz Okay.

Karl I'll take off the suit but I don't actually . . .

Franz I'll lend you something.

Karl I don't have a job.

Franz I'm sorry about that.

Karl We didn't get the contract. Rebuilding our school. But we didn't get the contract. It went to a company from the West. You understand these things better than us so – There's bids put in. But we don't have the words.

Franz Everything's changing.

Karl So there's not much for me over there.

Franz But still it's not working over here so – I know it's been fun but . . .

Karl I know. Two worlds.

Franz Oh no. Just –

Karl Yes. This is great here. I love your flat. Your kid. The shops, the . . . but that's not me. They're not mine. It's been great for a while. But I've got my own place over there. I'll find a job over there. Things'll look, I'll . . .

Franz If you're sure.

Karl You're right. I can't be you. I'll sort myself out. Now's the time to ask: Who am I?

Franz Would you like some cold sausage for the journey?

Karl Great.

Franz Oh.

Karl What?

Franz There's no sausage left.

Karl Oh well. Never mind.

Franz Drive safely.

Karl I'll do my best.

Five

East Berlin, 1991.

a.

Franz I had this taste in my mouth. I woke up up and it was there. Horrible. And I drank a lot of apple juice. But it was still there. And I chewed gum all morning during my meetings but it was getting stronger. And then I could smell it. And at first I thought it must be something with my car. I checked my car. It was okay. And then I realised the smell was everywhere. I was talking to Ulrike and she smelt of exhaust fumes. The park where I ate my sandwich . . . exhaust fumes. Everything was exhaust fumes. And I got into the car and I was going to go to the doctor but then suddenly I realised. So I didn't drive to the doctor's instead I carried on driving and I drove East, I – straight here. Because by then I had a really clear picture in my head of you doing it. Sealing the door with your old coat. Why did you do that, Karli? That was a really stupid thing to do.

Karl Why are you here Franzl?

Franz I'm here to help you.

Karl What about your boy?

Franz He's with his mother. I've got a few days. I've never really been East before so . . .

Karl I don't want your help.

Franz Yes. Well. You're going to get it anyway.

b.

Franz Good morning. Look at that. Plenty of meat.

Karl I di bat wesh ot.

Franz We're building you up.

Karl Ha bick Pust.

Franz Not in Russian Karli. I don't speak Russian. Speak German.

Karl Bi mant cure tif lo ni zpeck Noshun. Im bo spek Noshun une dat tis crall dut munner.

Franz Why are you doing that?

Karl Tebause me bant voo te ongertund oot ich drat.

Franz All right speak Russian if you want to.

Karl Ich koll.

Franz Just eat something.

Karl Ich munt fob lust e thunk.

Franz Come on just a –

Karl Ba.

Franz But you've got to –

Karl Gess pa. GESS PA. GESS PA.

Franz All right. All right. You speak Russian. You speak Russian go on.

Karl Ich jall.

Franz And I'll speak English and then we won't understand a thing the other one is saying. Is that what you want?

Karl Mant dfattink gure.

Franz Grere doo re Op creping Tranglise ung dos creatink Frosian unt paune intercrunds a frucky gord dem utter une spegs? Kis dat vat noo illly wass?

Karl Briddy oh.

Franz I bought really good sausage.

c.

Franz I'm going to wash you now.

Karl As frut ot yo prsk.

Franz Yes because actually Karli actually you're getting rather smelly.

Karl Me resi ka kam.

Franz But for me – while I'm looking after you –

Karl Re gut nod yemi.

Franz While I'm taking care of you then actually it would better for me if you were a bit cleaner.

Karl Struiverpo.

Franz So let's just . . . come on come on. That's better. Soon have you clean again.

Karl Rug gush.

Franz That's it. Hold still for me while I . . .

Karl Root ut dres vorg ite ye vanro.

Franz That's good. Really good.

Karl I dost: Root ut dres vorg ite ye vanro.

Franz And now we'll . . .

Karl Josten ye mo. Josten geo t me fallin ro.

Franz That's better already.

Karl Yam resying recout le rarb yat lo bin.

Franz Now if we . . .

Karl TE BIST NIST HE PRESTING AK LE.

Franz I'm only trying to help.

Karl GRUSS OD YA PI GRUSS OD.

Franz You've ruined it now.

Karl Ti kell.

Franz What am I supposed to do? No. Don't speak Russian. That's not doing any. Listen. Your society – a mistake. It was a wonderful. It was the best. The workers' and farmers' democracy. A beautiful. It went wrong. It fucked. It was a war. We won. The West. And you've got to change. You can't live. Okay so this new world isn't. Maybe it's a pile of. Okay – it's a pile of shit. But that's the world that we. And that's the world you've got to shop in and work in, make a family – so just you get on with. Take your history and your language and your – you wipe it – wash it away – because it was mistake – a sad tragic – and you begin again – begin again – invent yourself – with my help – begin again. Okay? Okay? OKAY?

Karl . . . Crotti. Me ro oker –

Franz No Russian.

Karl Bell o –

Franz What do you want? Tell me what you –

Karl . . . I want to go back.

Franz Yes?

Karl I want everything back.

Franz It's not –

Karl I want my world that I knew with my place in it and I want that now.

Franz But you have to change that's what –

Karl And I want a wall.

Franz Don't be –

Karl Yes. Between you and me. I want to wake up in the morning and find out they've put up a great wall between you and me and I want papers before we even see each other and every meeting we have I want someone watching I want a snoop following us noting everything down and everything scrutinised and I want –

Franz Don't be stupid.

Karl That's what I want.

Franz But it's fucking stupid.

Karl Well . . .

Franz Can I finish washing you?

Karl Your time's running out. The checkpoint's closing. Back behind the wall. Keep walking. Walk away or I'll shoot.

Franz Please let me wash you. Yes?

Karl *Report from Informant M July 28th: I watched them from my window. Twin A was taking a wet cloth and appeared to be washing Twin B. There have been no visitors to the flat for many days. From time to time loud music is played. They eat at irregular hours. An odd mixture of German, English and Russian is spoken. There is something very strange going on. These twins are up to something. I would recommend more detailed observation by professional surveillance operatives.*

Franz I'll finish washing you.

d.

Franz Look at this. You could do that. That's perfect for you.

Karl *He has offered a newspaper to his brother. He is suggesting employment with one of the many companies owned by shareholders largely resident in America. They seek to destabilise our way of life by employing low-paid and temporary workers while delivering maximum profits to the American shareholder. I am identifying his brother as an enemy of our country. Action should be taken.*

Franz I'll help with your application.

Karl *He is now suggesting . . .*

Franz Fuck's sake Karli. You've got to live.

Karl ... *His propaganda has been relentless. His brother is a weak man. He has suffered from depression and lacks a strong sense of purpose or of self. He has also now been persuaded by the propaganda. He is succumbing to the influence of America and international capitalism.*

Franz We'll fill out the form together.

e.

Franz *The main thing is motivating the team. What skills can you offer in . . . ?*

Karl I . . .

Franz *We have a frequent turnover of part-time and temporary staff. So with such a fluid workforce it's essential that the company offers a strong sense of ethos. How do you feel you will instill that sense of ethos into your team?*

Karl *Through regular team meetings I will set clear and achievable goals.*

Franz Good Karli yes.

Karl *With regular appraisals of both individual and team achievement I will identify the strengths, weaknesses, opportunities and threats that the franchise faces in delivering excellence to the consumer.*

Franz Brilliant. That's really good. Now – *What is your understanding of total quality management and how will you be implementing and delivering TQM in the day-to-day operation of the franchise?*

Karl *I will*, I'll –

Franz Yes?

Karl I will –

Franz It's all in the manual Karli. You don't have to actually think all you have to –

Karl I know.

Franz All you have to do is repeat back to them the section of TQM in the manual.

Karl I know that. So I –

Franz *What is your understanding of total quality management and how will you be implementing and delivering TQM in the day-to-day operation of the franchise?*

Karl I don't want to.

Franz You don't want to what?

Karl I'm not doing this. This is your language. This isn't my language. I hate this in my head. I don't want it. This company – this is a Western company.

Franz It's a German company.

Karl A West German company.

Franz There is no West Germany. That's gone. We're one. It's a German company.

Karl To you maybe. You're a Westie. But I look at that company and I see . . . Fuck your Germany. There's us and there's you. And you – my company – building company – we were good – we were decent workers – and then you bought it –

Franz Me? Don't you –

Karl One of you bought it and you stripped that company – you took our buildings, our land, our tools – you took them all and you sacked every single one of us – and you rolled in your forces and you occupied my country. There's no Germany. They're telling the kids now 'we're all one now' – well, we'll never be one and every child should know that.

Franz Where are you going?

Karl Out.

Franz Nothing's open it's –

Karl Thank you for trying Franzl. You're trying to help. You're a good person. But I sort of hate you. Which isn't right. Goodbye.

Franz We're one people.

f.

Franz *waits for* **Karl**. *A late-night game show is on the TV.*

. . .

Franz *falls asleep while waiting for* **Karl**.

. . .

Franz *wakes from his recurrent nightmare about the car crash.*

Franz Karli? Karli? Karl?

He has a piss and goes back to sleep.

. . .

The next morning **Franz** *eats a large meaty breakfast.*

. . .

Franz (*phone*)   Yes he was due to have an interview with you at eleven for the branch manager so I wondered if . . . okay thank you.

. . .

He tidies the room with great energy

. . .

He has fallen asleep. The phone is ringing He wakes and rushes over to the phone.

Franz Hello? Hello. Yes. Yes. Fuck.

He collects a few things and leaves.

Six

East Germany. A few days later.

Karl *is skinning a rabbit.*

Karl (Look at that. There's enough for two there. That's it. Wear your red scarf with pride. That means you're a member of the working class. And that means you have brothers across the world in every socialist nation. We love and respect work and join in whenever we can be helpful. Are you going to help me make a fire?)

Franz (*distant*)   Karli Karli Karli.

Karl *sings as he carries on the skinning. Enter* **Franz**.

Karl   Hello Franzl.

Franz   Have you hurt the boy?

Karl   Of course not.

Franz   That's the most precious thing to me that you didn't –

Karl   He's in the tent.

Franz   Let me see him.

Karl   He's just got off to –

Franz   I want to know he's all right.

Karl   He's all right. Tired. But that's the air. Coming from the lake. The air out here is so much fresher.

Franz *goes to check on the boy. Comes back with a red scarf.*

Franz   What's this?

Karl   He wanted to wear it.

Franz   It's a horrible thing.

Karl   He's proud to be a Young Pioneer. It's a very lonely life. But in the Pioneers you really do feel as though you've come together to build a better world.

Franz There is no better world. I want to burn this.

Karl We spend so much time in the city. When actually we have the most beautiful countryside in the world. This is the heart of Germany. The East.

Franz He's not your child.

Karl I feel much better in the forest. And so does he.

Franz He's my boy.

Karl Just a few years ago this was full of tents and cabins and thousands of young people would come here in the summer and there'd be sports and singing.

Franz I say where he goes. I decide what he does. I watch him. I take care of – so don't you –

Karl Bought now of course by a Westie. Three-year plan for development. And then it'll be holiday homes for the fat Westies and their fat wives and their grabbing children. So there's not much time to enjoy the peace. Do you want some rabbit?

Franz I'm not hungry.

Karl I caught it myself. You never know what you can do until you try, do you? There's not that much meat but . . . We can give the best bit to him and share the rest between you and me. What do you think?

Franz If you like.

Karl Franzl. You're tired.

Franz I've been driving for days, East, West, everywhere we ever . . .

Karl You sleep with your boy while I cook the rabbit.

Franz All right then.

Karl If you like it, we could stay out here.

Franz Forever?

Karl Maybe not forever. But a long time. Until the Westies arrive to occupy their holiday homes.

Franz I've got a meeting on Monday.

Karl Of course they're poisoning the lakes and the forests and so eventually they'll all be killed off.

Franz But – if you like – a couple of days. If that's what you want. A couple of days is fine. In the end we'll go back – but for now. The boy has to start school in a couple of months.

Karl He can learn all he needs to know out here with us.

Franz He has to learn the necessary skills to – He has to be prepared for the modern world. I'll go to him.

Karl That's right. You sleep. I'll cook.

Pause. **Karl** *prepares rabbit and sings while* **Franz** *goes into the tent. Enter* **Franz**.

Franz I want to kill you now.

Karl You've always wanted to do that. Why aren't you sleeping? Let me get on with my cooking in peace.

Franz My boy was asleep. But I've missed him so much. I really wanted to speak to him. Should I wake him? Of course waking him would be more about my emotional needs than his and really I should – shouldn't I? – put the emotional needs of the child above all else. But I have emotional needs. And I need to respect and listen to my needs also. So I decided – yes. I will wake my child. And I touched him on the shoulder and I whispered: 'Papa's here. Everything's all right now because Papa is here.' And my boy sat up in that sleeping bag and he, and he saluted me – like this – and he said, 'Be ready – be always ready.' And I said, 'What?' 'Now you say "always ready",' says the boy. 'I don't want to.' 'Say ready.' 'No'. 'Say ready.' 'Why should I say ready?' and he smiled and he laughed and he – I'll give you this – he looked so happy and he said, 'Silly. Don't you know it?

Karl (*salutes*) 'For peace and for socialism be ready – be always ready.' He likes saying it.

Franz I feel sick.

Karl I don't think actually he really understands yet what it means. But still he's young and in time –

Franz You're not taking him.

Karl Peace and socialism? What's wrong with that? That's what the world needs, isn't it? Peace and socialism?

Franz I'm going now. He's coming with me.

Karl There's rabbit.

Franz He doesn't he – we're going and we don't want to see you – we don't want to –

Karl Listen to that. He's calling my name.

Franz No he isn't.

Karl He wants me because he knows the one who –

Franz There's nothing. He's asleep.

Karl I'm going to him now.

Franz No you're not, you're –

Karl I know what's best.

Franz He can't have two fathers.

Karl He can he wants to he wants to know about my world.

Franz It's a dead world.

Karl *We want to become active builders of the socialist / society. By working hard to learn to learn through good deeds, we are helping socialism and the forces of peace throughout the world. At all times and in all places we oppose the incitement and the lies of the imperialists.*

Franz They're dead words coming out of your mouth – these are the stale – socialism – that's a lie – that didn't exist –

these tight poor lives of — you were deceiving yourselves — your world — listen to me — your world can't exist. There's only my world. Yes. This is my world. And you're going to live it.

Karl I hate your world.

Franz Make yourself. Like it. Take the blows. Fall in love with it. It's everything.

Karl Someone should go to that boy.

Franz He's quieter now.

Karl But he's having a nightmare. He's like you. He goes off but then he sees blood and screaming terrible things.

Franz He's quiet.

Karl But it's inside his head he sees —

Franz You don't know what's inside his head.

Karl Yes I do. Same as it was before with you and me. Now I see everything he sees, I feel it when he —

Franz No. See inside his — ? No. My boy. My boy. I'll raise him and he will be — you don't understand our life — you'll never — you stay over here —

Karl He wants me.

Franz Because you're too different to — you'll never have our skills — language — clothes — food — job — you can't take them —

Karl Listen to that.

Franz You're a thing — you're a less than human — you will never understand —

Karl He's mine.

Franz No. Fuck you. Fuck you.

Franz *knocks* **Karl** *to the ground.*

Franz Two of us? I don't want two of us. You're an echo. You're a shadow. You're a shitty little mirror that needs to be thrown away. I want just me. And my boy. In my world. You have to go.

Karl If you kill me.

Franz Leave us alone.

Karl I'll fight. Kill me.

Franz I don't want to.

Karl Yes you do. This is your world. Made in your image. Everything here you understand. I don't. Everything here you own. I don't. Everything is . . . So please. Only one.

Karl *gives* **Franz** *a pillow.*

Karl I will take from you. I've got nothing and all I can do is take so please you've got to . . .

Franz If you like.

Karl *lies down calmly and* **Franz** *holds the pillow over his face until he is dead.* **Franz** *sits. Looks at the body.*

Franz Are you dead?

Karl Yes.

Franz But you're still there.

Karl My body's here. That's all. There's no breath. Listen. You see? No heart. No pulse. Yes? Everything gone. Just flesh now.

Franz I thought somehow – stupid – you'd vanish. Just . . .

Karl I'll rot. In time. Bit of a stink but then . . . no one'll know. Pile of bones under a Westie's holiday home. They'll be watching their television and stuffing their children and they'll never know that I –

Franz I'd like you to stop talking now.

Karl If you like.

Franz If you're dead, I think you should be totally and utterly –

Karl I'll do whatever you want.

Franz I can't bear to see you. I can't bear to look at you. I don't want you there. I want. We're going to be one. I want you inside me. Swallow you down.

Karl That's your choice.

Franz Lie back and be quiet now. Dead man.

Karl Yes.

Karl *lies down.* **Franz** *chops off his hand. He lays the table. Starts to eat the hand. Retches. Carries on eating.*

Franz We are one.

Epilogue

a.

Franz I don't have German now. I look about me and everything I see is American. Juicer. Ioniser. Sun lamp. I don't know the German for these. In my head – all American.

Carly There's not much room in here. I used to have a great big condo. My husband sold cars. He made a good living. But then after a while no one bought cars any more. My husband went out in the sun all day. His skin turned to cancer so now it's just me. There's not much money so . . .

Franz It's okay.

Carly Honey I'm going to take off my clothes. My body isn't what it was. Everything hangs down and I . . .

Franz It's not a problem.

Carly Sometimes the guys find my body a bit too . . .

Franz That's okay.

Carly But I want to share myself with you so if you don't mind . . .

Franz I got a boy in college.

Carly That's great.

Franz Totally Californian. And he tells me the end's coming soon. The planet, atmosphere and the . . . he tells me we haven't got much time.

Carly Do you believe him?

Franz I don't think so.

Carly Let's go to bed.

b.

Carly What's the matter honey?
Franz Couldn't sleep.
Carly You had that nightmare again?
Franz Uh-huh.
Carly I'll hold you till you go off.
Franz I love you Carly.
Carly I love you Franzl. Try to sleep, okay?